Good Science—*That's Easy to Teach*

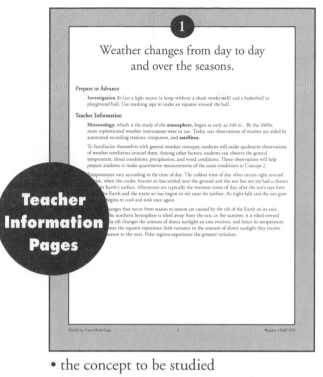

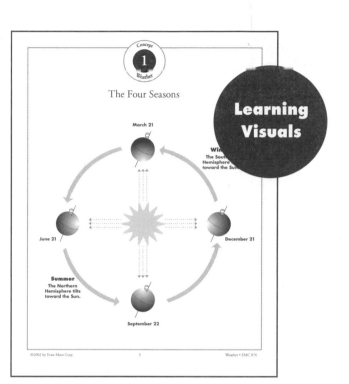

- the concept to be studied
- items to obtain or prepare in advance
- background information

• reproduce or make into transparency

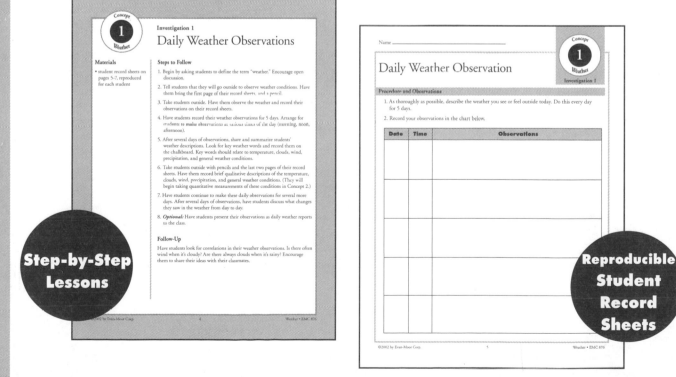

Weather changes from day to day and over the seasons.

Prepare in Advance

Investigation 3: Get a light source (a lamp without a shade works well) and a basketball or playground ball. Use masking tape to make an equator around the ball.

Teacher Information

Meteorology, which is the study of the **atmosphere,** began as early as 340 B.C.E. By the 1600s, more sophisticated weather instruments were in use. Today, our observations of weather are aided by automated recording stations, computers, and **satellites.**

To familiarize themselves with general weather concepts, students will make qualitative observations of weather conditions around them. Among other factors, students can observe the general temperature, cloud conditions, precipitation, and wind conditions. These observations will help prepare students to make quantitative measurements of the same conditions in Concept 2.

Temperatures vary according to the time of day. The coldest time of day often occurs right around sunrise, when the cooler, heavier air has settled near the ground and the Sun has not yet had a chance to warm Earth's surface. Afternoons are typically the warmest times of day, after the Sun's rays have heated Earth and the warm air has begun to stir near the surface. As night falls and the Sun goes away, air begins to cool and sink once again.

Weather changes that occur from season to season are caused by the tilt of Earth on its axis. In winter, the Northern Hemisphere is tilted away from the Sun; in the summer, it is tilted toward the Sun. This tilt changes the amount of direct sunlight an area receives, and hence its temperature. Locations near the equator experience little variance in the amount of direct sunlight they receive from one season to the next. Polar regions experience the greatest variation.

The Four Seasons

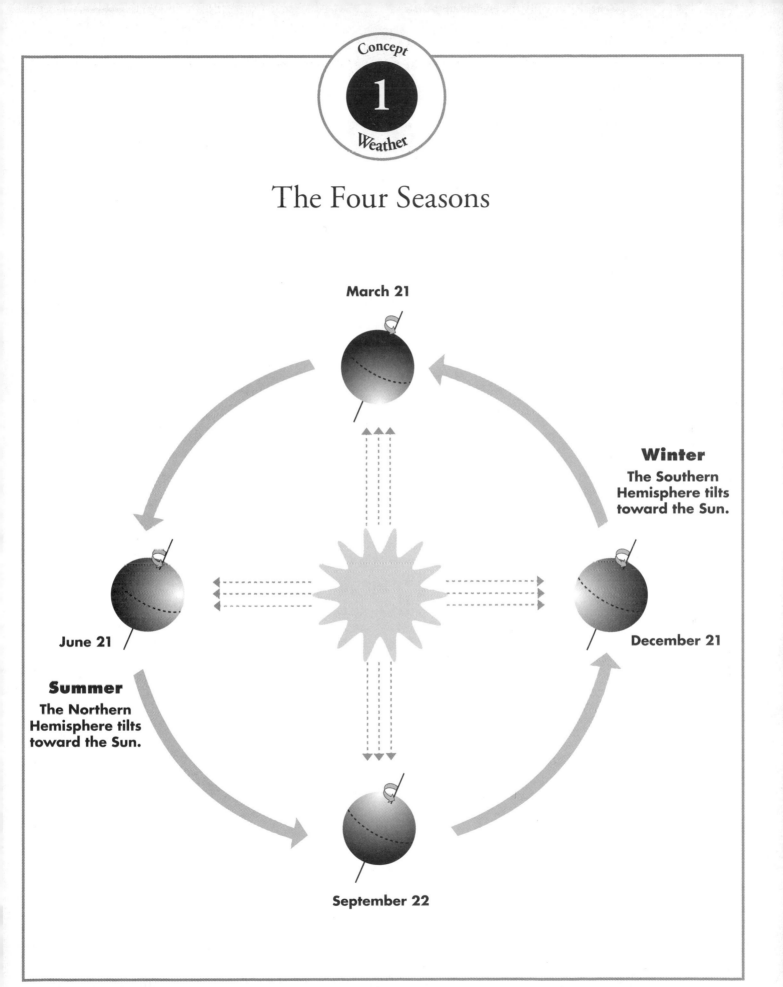

March 21

Winter
The Southern
Hemisphere tilts
toward the Sun.

June 21

December 21

Summer
The Northern
Hemisphere tilts
toward the Sun.

September 22

Investigation 1

Daily Weather Observations

Materials

- student record sheets on pages 5–7, reproduced for each student

Steps to Follow

1. Begin by asking students to define the term "weather." Encourage open discussion.

2. Tell students that they will go outside to observe weather conditions. Have them bring the first page of their record sheets and a pencil.

3. Take students outside. Have them observe the weather and record their observations on their record sheets.

4. Have students record their weather observations for five days. Arrange for students to make observations at various times of the day (morning, noon, and afternoon).

5. After several days of observations, share and summarize students' weather descriptions. Look for key weather words and record them on the chalkboard. Key words should relate to temperature, clouds, wind, precipitation, and general weather conditions.

6. Take students outside with pencils and the last two pages of their record sheets. Have them record brief qualitative descriptions of the temperature, clouds, wind, precipitation, and general weather conditions. (They will begin taking quantitative measurements of these conditions in Concept 2.)

7. Have students continue to make these daily observations for several more days. After several days of observations, have students discuss what changes they saw in the weather from day to day.

8. *Optional:* Have students present their observations as daily weather reports to the class.

Follow-Up

Have students look for correlations in their weather observations. Is there often wind when it's cloudy? Are there always clouds when it's rainy? Encourage them to share their ideas with their classmates.

Concept

1

Weather

Investigation 1

Daily Weather Observations

Procedure and Observations

1. As thoroughly as possible, describe the weather you see or feel outside today. Do this every day for five days.

2. Record your observations on the chart below.

Date	Time	Observations

3. Describe the weather for five days, using the categories shown below.

4. Record your data on the charts below.

Date_____ Time_____

Condition	Observations
Temperature	
Clouds	
Precipitation	
Wind	
General Conditions	

Date_____ Time_____

Condition	Observations
Temperature	
Clouds	
Precipitation	
Wind	
General Conditions	

Date_____ Time_____

Condition	Observations
Temperature	
Clouds	
Precipitation	
Wind	
General Conditions	

Date_____ Time_____

Condition	Observations
Temperature	
Clouds	
Precipitation	
Wind	
General Conditions	

Date_____ Time_____

Condition	Observations
Temperature	
Clouds	
Precipitation	
Wind	
General Conditions	

Concept 1 Weather

Investigation 2

Morning and Afternoon Weather

Materials

- student record sheets on pages 9 and 10, reproduced for each student

Steps to Follow

1. Review with students their record sheets with daily weather charts from Investigation 1. Ask them if they notice any differences between observations they made in the morning and those they made in the afternoon. (Temperatures were probably higher in the afternoon.)

2. For the next five days, take students outside twice a day to observe and describe the weather, once in the morning and once in the afternoon. Have them record their observations on their record sheets.

3. After five days of observations, have students share their findings.

4. Ask students when the coolest and warmest parts of the day usually are. (Mornings are normally cooler than afternoons.)

5. Ask students to offer explanations for their observations. (As the Sun warms Earth's surface, the air begins to heat up. In the afternoon, the Sun has had a chance to warm Earth for a while. In the morning, the air has been cooling all night.)

6. Discuss any other trends students might have noticed. (Wind picking up in the afternoons, clouds clearing or forming in the afternoons, rain falling in the afternoons, etc.).

Follow-Up

Have students create their own weather charts in which to record weather data at home. Have them share their observations the next day in class.

Name _____

Morning and Afternoon Weather

Procedure and Observations

1. Describe the weather in the morning and the afternoon for five days.

2. Record your observations on the charts below.

Date_____

Condition	Morning Observations	Afternoon Observations
Temperature		
Clouds		
Precipitation		
Wind		
General Conditions		

Date_____

Condition	Morning Observations	Afternoon Observations
Temperature		
Clouds		
Precipitation		
Wind		
General Conditions		

Date_____

Condition	Morning Observations	Afternoon Observations
Temperature		
Clouds		
Precipitation		
Wind		
General Conditions		

Date_____

Condition	Morning Observations	Afternoon Observations
Temperature		
Clouds		
Precipitation		
Wind		
General Conditions		

Date_____

Condition	Morning Observations	Afternoon Observations
Temperature		
Clouds		
Precipitation		
Wind		
General Conditions		

Concept 1 Weather

Investigation 3

Seasons

Materials

See advance preparation on page 2.

• student record sheets on pages 12 and 13, reproduced for each student

• ball with "equator"

Steps to Follow

1. Place a light source on a desk in the middle of the room. Turn the lamp on. Turn the classroom lights off.

2. Hold the ball near the lamp so that only half of it is illuminated. (The equator should be parallel with the floor.) Explain that in this model, the ball represents Earth and the lamp represents the Sun. Point out that the area above the tape represents the Northern Hemisphere (the one that contains the United States) and that the area below the tape represents the Southern Hemisphere.

3. Rotate the ball around its own vertical axis. (Looking at the top of the ball, it would spin in a counterclockwise direction.) Explain that Earth makes a complete rotation (one spin) in 24 hours.

4. Explain that Earth also revolves around the Sun, making one complete trip each year. Use the ball and lamp to model how Earth revolves around the Sun.

5. Now explain that Earth's axis is actually tilted about 23° in relation to its orbit around the Sun. Tilt the top of the ball slightly to your left so that the taped "equator" is no longer parallel with the floor. Rotate the ball around on its own "axis" to demonstrate this tilt.

6. Mark off four evenly-spaced spots in a circle around the lamp. These will represent the starting points of the four seasons.

7. Still holding the ball at the same tilt, walk slowly around the circle. Stop at each of the four spots you marked and discuss the relationship of the Northern Hemisphere to the sunlight. (At one position in the circle, the Northern Hemisphere is tilted toward the Sun and the Sun's rays fall directly on it. At an opposite position in the circle, the Northern Hemisphere points away from the Sun.)

8. Ask students to speculate as to which position corresponds to which season in the Northern Hemisphere. (When sunlight most directly hits the ball above the equator, it's summer in the Northern Hemisphere. When sunlight most directly hits below the equator, it's winter in the Northern Hemisphere. Spring and fall occur somewhere in between.)

9. Have students complete their record sheets.

Seasons

Procedure and Observations

1. Watch as your teacher models the revolution of Earth around the Sun. Use your observations to answer the questions below.

2. When the Sun's rays are shining directly on the Northern Hemisphere, what are they doing in the Southern Hemisphere?

   _____

   _____

3. When the Sun's rays are shining directly on the Southern Hemisphere, what are they doing in the Northern Hemisphere?

   _____

   _____

Conclusions

4. Why is it warmer in the Northern Hemisphere during our summer?

   _____

   _____

5. Why is it cooler in the Northern Hemisphere during our winter?

   _____

   _____

6. What did you learn about spring and fall from the model? Explain what you learned in terms of the Sun's rays falling on Earth.

   _____

   _____

   _____

Procedure and Observations

7. Here is a map showing the locations and average high temperatures for three different cities in July and January.

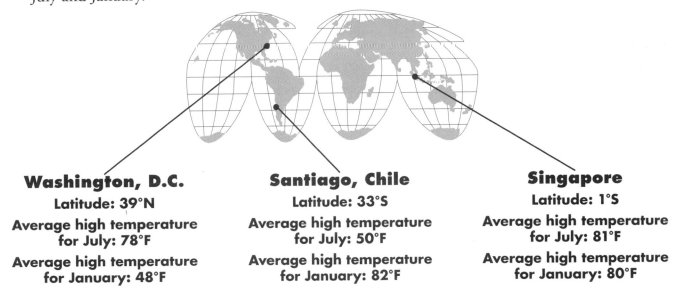

Washington, D.C.
Latitude: 39°N
Average high temperature
for July: 78°F
Average high temperature
for January: 48°F

Santiago, Chile
Latitude: 33°S
Average high temperature
for July: 50°F
Average high temperature
for January: 82°F

Singapore
Latitude: 1°S
Average high temperature
for July: 81°F
Average high temperature
for January: 80°F

8. Study the map. How can you explain the fact that Santiago's summer and winter temperatures are opposite those of Washington, D.C.?

_____

_____

9. Calculate the temperature range between the seasons for each city by subtracting the lower temperature from the higher temperature.

City	Range
Singapore	
Washington, D.C.	
Santiago, Chile	

10. How can you explain the fact that the temperature range for Singapore is very small?

_____

_____

Weather conditions can be described in measurable quantities.

Prepare in Advance

Investigation 1: Prepare a poster-size version of the *Daily Weather Chart* found on page 16. Post the chart on the classroom wall where all students can see it. You will need to create more copies of the chart as it gets filled up with data.

Investigation 2: Prepare a poster-size bird's-eye view map of the school grounds. Maps can include various features from the school grounds, including soccer fields, basketball courts, trees, the flagpole, and outdoor hallways.

Investigation 3: Calibrate the classroom barometer using local barometric pressure data. The Weather Channel (www.weather.com) and the National Weather Service (www.nws.noaa.gov) both have regional sites that give hourly barometric pressure readings.

Investigation 4: Walk around your school grounds to determine the best places to observe wind direction. Hopefully, the school flag is unobstructed by trees and will serve this purpose well. Using a ruler, compass, and chalk, set up a cardinal and intermediate direction compass underneath the school flag.

Investigation 5: Search for pictures of anemometers on Internet sites such as Wind and Weather (www.windandweather.com) to show students what they look like.

Investigation 6: Purchase a rain gauge from a local hardware store. Search the school grounds for a proper, unobstructed place to put up the rain gauge.

Investigation 7: You will need several strips of cobalt paper. These may be ordered from educational science supply companies.

Teacher Information

All matter is made up of atoms. These atoms have kinetic energy because they are moving or vibrating. Temperature is a measure of the average kinetic energy of matter. Air temperature can be measured using a **thermometer.** The two most common scales of temperature are the Fahrenheit scale (used commonly in the United States) and the Celsius scale (used elsewhere in the world, and by scientists everywhere).

At any given time, you may find a variety of temperatures around the school grounds. The temperature in any specific area is determined by the amount of direct sunlight shining on it, whether or not it is protected by shade, how windy it is, what the moisture level is, and what the type and color of surfaces are. These factors explain why a school's blacktop might be 80°F at the same time a grassy patch beneath a bush is only 62°F.

Air is matter, and therefore has weight and exerts pressure. The pressure exerted by the air over Earth is constant, but changes locally. **Air pressure** at any one spot can be measured using a **barometer.** Cool, sinking air is usually associated with high pressure. Warm, rising air is usually associated with low pressure. Generally speaking, high pressure brings fair weather, while low pressure brings showers or storms.

Wind direction is always expressed as the direction *from which* the wind blows. If there is a north wind, then the wind is blowing from the north. Wind is simply the movement of air from one place to another. Air moves from areas of higher pressure to areas of lower pressure.

The **Beaufort Wind Scale** is a guide for estimating wind speed. By comparing actual outdoor observations (such as the movement of leaves, trees, loose paper, and so on) to the information on the Beaufort Wind Scale, the observer can determine an estimated wind speed in miles per hour. Because wind often increases in the afternoon, it is usually beneficial to estimate wind speed twice a day.

Humidity is the measure of how much moisture or **water vapor** is in the air. Water vapor is simply water in its gaseous state. Warmer air can hold more water vapor than cooler air.

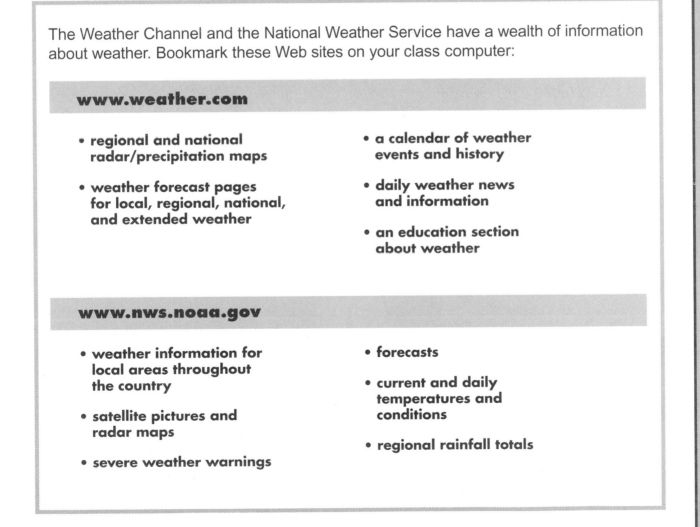

The Weather Channel and the National Weather Service have a wealth of information about weather. Bookmark these Web sites on your class computer:

www.weather.com

- regional and national radar/precipitation maps
- weather forecast pages for local, regional, national, and extended weather

- a calendar of weather events and history
- daily weather news and information
- an education section about weather

www.nws.noaa.gov

- weather information for local areas throughout the country
- satellite pictures and radar maps
- severe weather warnings

- forecasts
- current and daily temperatures and conditions
- regional rainfall totals

Daily Weather Chart

		Date	Date	Date	Date	Date
Temperature (°F)	A.M.					
	P.M.					
Air Pressure (in.)	A.M.					
	P.M.					
Wind Direction	A.M.					
	P.M.					
Wind Speed (mph)	A.M.					
	P.M.					
Rainfall (in. or cm)						
Humidity (1–5)						
Cloud Coverage	A.M.					
	P.M.					
Cloud Types	A.M.					
	P.M.					
Prediction						

Thermometer

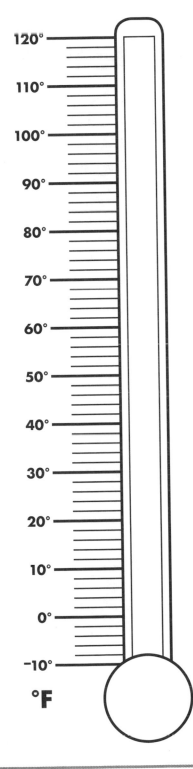

120°
110°
100°
90°
80°
70°
60°
50°
40°
30°
20°
10°
0°
-10°

°F

Beaufort Wind Scale

Observation	Name of Wind	Miles per Hour	Symbol
Smoke goes straight up	Calm	Less than 1	
Smoke moves, but wind vane does not	Light air	1–3	
Leaves rustle, wind vane moves, wind felt on face	Light breeze	4–7	
Leaves and small twigs move constantly, wind extends light flag	Gentle breeze	8–12	
Dust raised, dead leaves and loose paper blow about, small branches move	Moderate breeze	13–18	
Small trees sway, small waves crest on lakes or streams	Fresh breeze	19–24	
Large branches move constantly, wind howls around eaves, wires on telephone poles hum	Strong breeze	25–31	
Large trees sway, walking against wind is inconvenient	Moderate or near gale	32–38	
Twigs break off trees, walking against wind is difficult	Gale or fresh gale	39–46	
Branches break off trees, loose bricks blown off chimneys, shingles blown off	Strong gale	47–54	
Trees snap or are uprooted, considerable damage to buildings is possible	Whole gale or storm	55–63	
Widespread damage to buildings	Violent storm	64–72	
General destruction	Hurricane	73 and over	

Rain Gauge

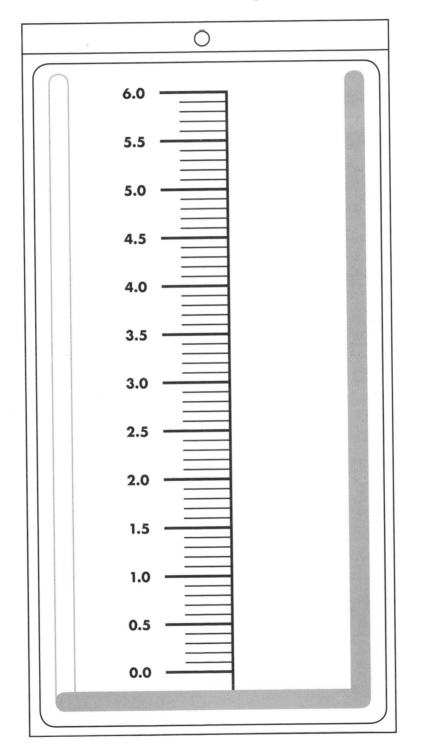

Concept
2
Weather

Investigation 1

Temperature

Materials

See advance preparation on page 14.

- student record sheet on page 21, reproduced for each student
- overhead transparency of *Thermometer* on page 17
- *Daily Weather Chart* on page 16
- 5 thermometers
- erasable markers

Steps to Follow

1. Ask students to guess what the temperature in the room is. Use an actual thermometer to measure the temperature, and tell the class the temperature.

2. Ask students if they think the temperature is different in various locations in the room, such as on the floor, at the windowsill, in a desk, near the ceiling, and on the door.

3. Have students place a thermometer in five chosen locations. Leave the thermometers in place for three or more minutes.

4. While waiting, use the *Thermometer* transparency to familiarize students with the instrument.

5. Explain that as the air around the thermometer grows warmer, the liquid inside expands and moves up the glass. As the air cools, the liquid contracts and moves down.

6. Using an erasable marker, color in the thermometer to indicate a specific temperature. Ask the students to read the temperature. Repeat several times with various temperatures.

7. Invite students to read the temperatures of the thermometers that were placed around the classroom earlier. Write these temperatures and their locations on the board. Have students record the data on their record sheets.

8. Discuss possible causes of the temperature differences seen around the room (warm air rising, drafts near windows, direct sunlight, etc.).

9. Have students record temperatures in the shade outside. They should do this twice a day—once in the morning and once just before school is out—for five days, and they should take each reading from the same location. Have students record their data on their record sheets.

10. Show students the *Daily Weather Chart* you've prepared. Explain that students will use it to collect weather data over the next several weeks. Tell students that they will begin by collecting temperature data.

11. Have different weather monitors observe and record outside temperatures twice a day for several weeks. Tell them to enter the data on the *Daily Weather Chart* posted on a classroom wall.

Temperature

Procedure and Observations

1. With your classmates, place one thermometer at each of five different locations around the classroom. Leave them there for several minutes.

2. Record the temperatures at each of the five different locations on the chart below.

Classroom Location	Temperature (°F)

3. Record the morning (A.M.) and afternoon (P.M.) temperatures outside your classroom for five days. Record the data on the chart below.

Temperature (°F)

Outdoor Location	Day 1 Date:		Day 2 Date:		Day 3 Date:		Day 4 Date:		Day 5 Date:	
	A.M.	P.M.	A.M.	P.M.	A.M.	P.M.	A.M.	P.M.	A.M.	P.M.

Investigation 2

Microclimates

Materials

See advance preparation on page 14.

- student record sheet on page 23, reproduced for each student
- thermometers
- bird's-eye view map of the school
- pencils
- stopwatch
- whistle

Steps to Follow

1. As needed, review with students how to read a thermometer.

2. Show students the bird's-eye view map of the school you prepared. Make a list of all the outdoor locations where students want to take temperature readings.

3. Divide students into small groups. Distribute a thermometer to each group. Assign one of the locations on the list to each group.

4. Have teams use their thermometers to take temperature readings at the outdoor locations. They should leave their thermometers undisturbed in the assigned location for three minutes.

5. After three minutes, blow a whistle. The students should read the temperatures and return to the classroom.

6. As a class, record the temperatures at their correct locations on the bird's-eye view map. Remember to label the date and time.

7. Find the lowest and highest temperatures. Write the temperature range on the chalkboard. Subtract the lowest from the highest reading and write the difference on the board.

8. Discuss with the class why the temperatures might have varied so dramatically from one location to the next (shady v. sunlit areas, windy v. protected areas, etc.).

9. Explain that a "microclimate" is an area that has its own specific weather conditions, like temperature. Invite students to name some microclimates they identified within their school grounds, based on the data they collected.

Follow-Up

Repeat the activity at various times, including morning, afternoon, a sunny day, a cloudy day, a stormy day, and during the different seasons. Compare the results. On which days were the greatest number of microclimates identified?

Name _____

Microclimates

Procedure and Observations

1. Determine the temperature of the area assigned to your team. Record the reading on the first line of the chart below. On the lines below that, record the temperatures found by the other teams in your class.

Location	Temperature (°F)

2. Which location had the warmest temperature, and what was the temperature?

Location _____   **Temperature (°F)** _____

3. Which location had the coolest temperature, and what was the temperature?

Location _____   **Temperature (°F)** _____

Conclusion

4. Why do you think the temperatures varied so much, even though they were all taken at the same time of day?

_____

_____

_____

Investigation 3

Air Pressure

Materials

See advance preparation on page 14.

- student record sheet on page 25, reproduced for each student
- *Daily Weather Chart* on page 16
- large round balloon or rubber sheet
- wide-mouthed glass jar
- rubber band
- classroom barometer, calibrated to local conditions

Steps to Follow

1. Hold a class discussion on air pressure. Explain that air has weight and that it exerts pressure on things around it, including Earth's surface.

2. Tell students that a special instrument, called a **barometer**, is used to measure air pressure. Air pressure is also called **barometric pressure**.

3. Show students the classroom barometer. Explain how to read it. (It may show air pressure in inches or millibars. Explain that the inches scale refers to inches of mercury, a number system based on an old barometer. Millibars are the metric unit of measurement for barometric pressure.)

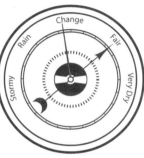

4. Demonstrate the concept of how a barometer works. Place the barometer in a glass jar. Cut the open end off the balloon and stretch it tightly over the top of the jar. Seal the balloon with a rubber band.

5. Have students observe the pressure reading on the barometer.

6. Now press down on the balloon and have students observe what happens to the barometer needle. (It moves to indicate a higher pressure.)

7. Explain that as you press down on the balloon, the air molecules inside the jar are pressed closer together, and so they exert more pressure on the barometer. This is why the needle indicated a greater pressure.

8. Remove the barometer from the jar and place it in a central location where everyone can read it.

9. Have students measure air pressure changes in the mornings and afternoons for five days and record the data on their record sheets. Also have them note the weather conditions during these times. (Students should note a connection between low barometric pressure and stormy weather.)

10. Continue to have different weather monitors observe and record barometric pressure twice a day for several weeks. Tell them to enter the data on the *Daily Weather Chart* posted on a classroom wall.

Name _____

Air Pressure

Procedure and Observations

1. Use the classroom barometer to measure air pressure in the mornings and afternoons for five days. Record your data on the chart below. Also record the general weather conditions on each of those days.

Day	Date	Time	Air Pressure (in.)	General Weather Conditions
1		morning		
		afternoon		
2		morning		
		afternoon		
3		morning		
		afternoon		
4		morning		
		afternoon		
5		morning		
		afternoon		

Conclusions

2. What happened to the barometric pressure over the course of five days?

_____

_____

_____

3. Do you notice any weather patterns associated with higher or lower air pressure?

_____

_____

_____

Concept 2 — Weather

Investigation 4

Wind Direction

Materials

See advance preparation on page 14.

- student record sheet on page 27, reproduced for each student
- *Daily Weather Chart* on page 16
- compasses
- school flag or windsock

Steps to Follow

1. Tell students that they will be adding wind direction data to the *Daily Weather Chart*.

2. Draw a wind direction compass on the chalkboard and explain to students the cardinal and intermediate wind directions.

3. Explain to students that wind direction is always expressed as the direction the wind blows from; for example, a north wind blows from the north.

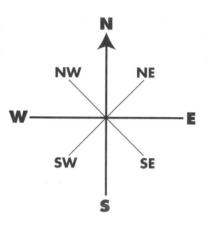

4. Take the class outside and give each student a compass. Review with students the cardinal and intermediate directions.

5. Explain to students that wind direction can be determined by a wind vane, wind sock, the school flag, or even bushes and trees.

6. Ask students which direction they think the wind is coming from. Discuss what clues are needed to determine wind direction.

7. Take students over to the wind direction compass already set up underneath the school flag. Show students the compass you used to mark these directions. Point out cardinal and intermediate wind directions from where the students are standing.

8. Explain that when there is a north wind, meaning the wind is blowing from the north, the flag will be flapping toward the south. Trees and bushes also sway in the opposite direction from which the wind blows.

9. Invite students to look up at the flag and determine which direction the wind is blowing from. Have them record this direction on their record sheets.

10. Have students use the flag to record wind direction for the next five days. They should record their data on the record sheets.

11. Continue to have different weather monitors observe and record wind direction twice a day for several weeks. Tell them to enter the data on the *Daily Weather Chart*.

Concept

2

Weather

Investigation 4

Wind Direction

Procedure and Observations

1. Go outside with your teacher and follow her instructions for reading a compass.

2. Label the wind direction finder.

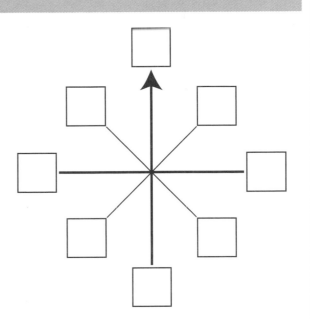

3. What direction is the wind blowing from today?

_____

4. Record the wind direction for five days.

	Day 1	Day 2	Day 3	Day 4	Day 5
	Date:	Date:	Date:	Date:	Date:
Wind Direction					

Conclusions

5. How did the wind direction change over five days?

_____

_____

6. What other outside objects can you use to determine wind direction?

_____

_____

_____

Concept 2 Weather

Investigation 5

Wind Speed

Materials

See advance preparation on page 14.

• student record sheet on page 29, reproduced for each student

• overhead transparency of the *Beaufort Wind Scale* on page 18

• *Daily Weather Chart* on page 16

• pictures of various wind speed instruments

Steps to Follow

1. Explain to students how wind speed is measured by anemometers and wind speed meters. (Most anemometers have a mechanism that catches the wind as it blows past. The force of the wind is then calculated mechanically or electronically.) Show pictures of various wind speed instruments.

2. Show the overhead transparency of the *Beaufort Wind Scale*. Tell students that wind speed can be estimated using this scale. Go over the descriptions for each category.

3. Assign individual students to draw sample pictures for three of the 13 categories on the wind scale (Calm, Light Air, Light Breeze, etc.). Each picture should also include the wind speed (in mph) and the wind category's label.

4. Choose the easiest to read or clearest picture drawn for each category. Post them in order (least to greatest wind speed) on a piece of chart paper, and post the paper next to the *Daily Weather Chart*.

5. Take students outside and have them practice using the *Beaufort Wind Scale* to estimate wind speed. For the most accurate data, they should make their observations in an open area that is not obstructed by large trees or buildings. Have students make daily recording for five days and record their data on the record sheets.

6. Select weather monitors to measure wind speed twice a day for several weeks. Tell them to enter the data on the *Daily Weather Chart*.

Follow-Up

Consider purchasing or making an anemometer or wind speed meter. Use the instrument to record wind speeds. Compare these readings to those of the *Beaufort Wind Scale*. Also compare local wind speed readings from the National Weather Service (www.nws.noaa.gov) with the class estimations.

Name _____

Wind Speed

Procedure and Observations

1. In the spaces below, illustrate the three *Beaufort Wind Scale* wind speeds assigned to you by your teacher. Label each drawing with its category title (Calm, Light Air, etc.) and its wind speed in miles per hour.

2. Go outside and practice using the *Beaufort Wind Scale* to estimate wind speed.

3. According to the *Beaufort Wind Scale*, what is the wind speed today?

_____

4. What object or objects did you look at to help determine wind speed?

_____

_____

_____

5. Use the *Beaufort Wind Scale* to record wind speed for five days. Record your data on the chart below.

	Day 1	Day 2	Day 3	Day 4	Day 5
	Date:	Date:	Date:	Date:	Date:
Wind Speed (mph)					

Concept **2** Weather

Investigation 6

Measuring Rainfall

Materials

See advance preparation on page 14.

- student record sheet on page 31, reproduced for each student
- overhead transparency of *Rain Gauge* on page 19
- *Daily Weather Chart* on page 16
- rain gauge
- water
- erasable markers

Steps to Follow

1. On a rainy day, take students to a hallway or breezeway and invite them to watch and describe the rain.

2. Ask students how much rain is falling and how they can find out the exact amount.

3. Bring students back to class and show them a rain gauge. Explain that if the rain gauge is placed correctly outside, it can measure the amount of rain that falls in a certain amount of time.

4. Using the *Rain Gauge* transparency, label it according to the scale used on your rain gauge (inches or centimeters). Teach students to read various rainfall totals by coloring in the rain gauge at different levels on the transparency.

5. Fill the actual rain gauge with varying amounts of water. Walk around with the filled rain gauge and ask students to name the rainfall amounts.

6. With the class in tow, post the rain gauge outside in an open area away from trees or buildings. The top of a fence works well.

7. Have students check the rain gauge each day for five days and record their data on their record sheets. Make sure students empty the gauge after each reading.

8. Assign weather monitors to check and record rainfall every day for the next several weeks. Have the monitors record the rainfall amounts on the *Daily Weather Chart*. After each rainfall recording, the weather monitors should empty the rain gauge.

Follow-Up

Invite students and their families to set up rain gauges at their homes. Have students record rainfall totals at home and compare them with the totals measured at school. Also compare school rainfall totals for each storm with those posted for your city, or one nearby, through the National Weather Service Web site (www.nws.noaa.gov).

Name _____

Measuring Rainfall

Procedure and Observations

1. Help your teacher to set up the rain gauge in an unobstructed area outside.

2. Each day for five days, observe the rain gauge and record any rainfall measurements on the chart below.

3. After each recording, dump out the water from the rain gauge.

	Day 1 Date:	**Day 2** Date:	**Day 3** Date:	**Day 4** Date:	**Day 5** Date:
Rainfall Amount (in. or cm)					

Conclusion

4. Describe the area where your class set up the rain gauge. Why was this a good location for it?

_____

_____

_____

_____

Investigation 7

Humidity

Materials

See advance preparation on page 14.

- student record sheet on page 33, reproduced for each student
- *Daily Weather Chart* on page 16
- cobalt paper
- hot plate
- glass beaker
- water

Steps to Follow

1. Show the class a piece of dry cobalt paper, which should be blue. Explain that the cobalt paper has a special chemical on it to measure humidity, or the amount of moisture in the air.

   Caution: Warn students not to put the cobalt paper in their mouths.

2. Demonstrate how cobalt paper works: Heat water in a beaker on a hot plate until the water boils. Ask students to describe what they see above the beaker (steam or water vapor). Explain that steam is water in the air.

3. Place a piece of cobalt paper several feet above the beaker and slowly bring it down toward the steam until it begins to turn pink. Challenge students to explain their observations. Lead students to conclude that as cobalt paper comes into contact with moisture, it turns pink. For this reason, it can be used as an indicator for humidity.

4. When you have completed the demonstration, put the piece of cobalt paper on a table to dry. The cobalt paper will turn back to blue as it dries. Ask the class to describe why this happens. (As the moisture leaves the paper, it turns blue again.)

5. Tell students that they are now going to measure the humidity of the air.

6. Divide students into small groups. Give each group a strip of cobalt paper. (Make sure students' hands are dry before they handle the cobalt paper.)

7. Lead students outside and have them set their strips of cobalt paper in a shady spot and observe them for several minutes. Have them record their observations on their record sheets.

8. Instruct students to take humidity readings every day for the next five days and record their observations on their record sheets.

9. Assign weather monitors to measure relative humidity levels every day for the next several weeks. Have them record the readings (1–5) on the *Daily Weather Chart*.

Follow-Up

Consider purchasing or making a class hygrometer, an instrument for measuring humidity. Once the hygrometer is set up, add quantitative humidity level readings to the *Daily Weather Chart*.

Name _____

Humidity

Procedure and Observations

1. Describe a piece of dry cobalt paper.

   _____

2. Describe what happens to the cobalt paper as your teacher holds it over a beaker of boiling water.

   _____

3. Take your piece of cobalt paper outside. Set it in a shady spot for several minutes. Did it change in any way? Describe any changes you saw.

   _____

   _____

4. Use your cobalt paper strip to measure humidity levels for the next five days. (Rate the color of your cobalt paper on a scale of 1 to 5, with 1 being very blue and 5 being very pink.) Record your data on the chart below. Also record the general weather conditions on that day.

	Day 1 Date:	Day 2 Date:	Day 3 Date:	Day 4 Date:	Day 5 Date:
Humidity Level (1–5)					
General Weather Conditions					

Conclusions

5. How did humidity levels change over the course of five days?

   _____

6. How did the humidity levels compare to general weather conditions? Do you notice any patterns?

   _____

   _____

Water circulates throughout Earth's atmosphere.

Prepare in Advance

Investigation 3: Try the cloud experiment on your own. Make sure the amount of water and matches is enough to create a cloud. Ask the class ahead of time to save and bring to school clear plastic bottles until you have about a dozen. Students can also bring flashlights from home.

Investigation 4: Try this experiment with another adult first. Make sure you are wearing an oven mitt when you hold the pie plate, and don't hold the plate too close to the steaming kettle. Decide what a safe viewing distance should be for students.

Teacher Information

Evaporation is the change in state of a liquid to a gas. Liquid water evaporates to form water vapor, an invisible gas. Evaporation rate is influenced by wind, sunlight, temperature, and surface area.

Condensation is the opposite of evaporation; it is the change in state of a gas to a liquid. When water vapor in the air cools, it condenses around dust particles in the air, forming tiny water droplets that are suspended in clouds. Eventually these droplets become heavy enough to fall to the Earth as **precipitation.** Depending on the temperature, precipitation can fall as rain, snow, sleet, or hail.

Water is constantly being recycled on our planet through the **water cycle.** Water evaporates into the atmosphere, where it cools and condenses to form clouds. The clouds drop precipitation, which collects in bodies of water, such as oceans, lakes, rivers, streams, and ponds. Once the water is back on Earth, it will eventually evaporate, thus continuing the water cycle. New water is not created; in fact, water that falls as rain today might be the same water that dinosaurs drank millions of years ago.

The Water Cycle

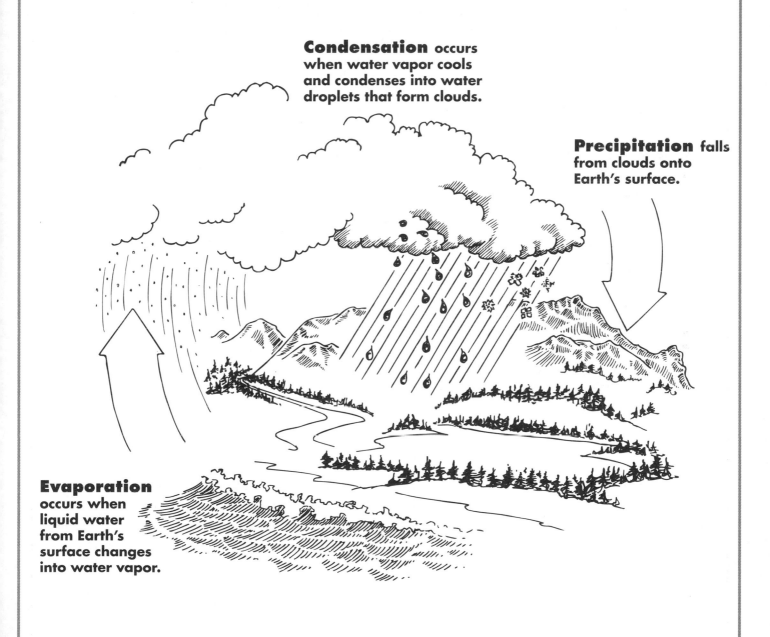

Condensation occurs when water vapor cools and condenses into water droplets that form clouds.

Precipitation falls from clouds onto Earth's surface.

Evaporation occurs when liquid water from Earth's surface changes into water vapor.

Concept 3 Weather

Investigation 1

Evaporation

Materials

- student record sheets on pages 37 and 38, reproduced for each student
- spray bottle filled with water
- fan
- small portable chalkboard
- stopwatch

Steps to Follow

1. Ask students if they know what happens to the water in puddles on a hot day. (It evaporates.) Tell them that, in this investigation, they will look at the process of **evaporation.**

2. Take a spray bottle filled with water and mist the chalkboard, or any other surface that will make the water droplets visible. Use three full squirts, about 6 inches from the surface.

3. Have a student volunteer use a stopwatch to time how long it takes for the water spots to disappear from the surface.

4. Record the time in minutes and seconds on the board. Have students record the number on their record sheets.

5. Ask the class if they can think of any way to make the same amount of water disappear faster. (Someone may suggest wind.)

6. Repeat the procedure, except this time hold a fan over the misted surface.

7. Again, record the data on the board, and have students record it on their record sheets.

8. Again, ask if there's any way to make the same amount of water disappear even faster. (Someone may suggest sunlight.)

9. Take the class outside on a sunny day. Hold the board in direct sunlight. Spray the chalkboard with the same amount of water and time the evaporation rate.

10. Repeat this activity again, but this time spray concrete or blacktop that is in direct sunlight. Record all evaporation rate data.

11. Explain to the class that when the water disappears, it actually turns into water vapor, an invisible gas, and enters the air. This process is called **evaporation.** Review with students which variables affected the evaporation rate.

Follow-Up

If possible, repeat the investigation early in the morning when it is cold, and late in the afternoon when it is warm. Note the differences in evaporation rates. Also try this experiment on various surfaces—including different paint colors—to see if evaporation rates are affected.

Name _____

Concept

3

Weather

Investigation 1

Evaporation

Procedure and Observations

1. With your teacher and the rest of the class, time how long it takes misted water to disappear from the surfaces you sprayed it on.

2. Record your data on the chart below.

Location	Evaporation Rate (min., sec.)
Inside	
Inside with Fan	
Outside	
Outside on Sidewalk or Blacktop	

3. Graph the evaporation rates for each location on the bar graph below.

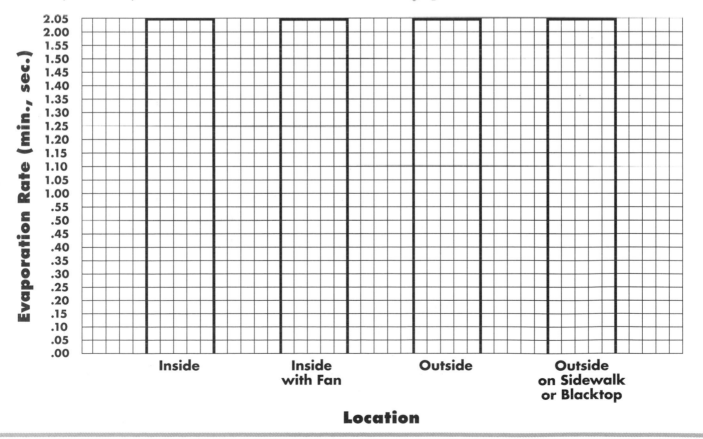

Conclusions

4. Define *evaporation*. Where did the water go?

_____

_____

_____

_____

_____

5. Why do you think the evaporation rates were different in each location? What were the factors involved in different evaporation rates?

_____

_____

_____

_____

_____

6. How can you make the same amount of water evaporate faster? Slower? What other factors could change the rate of evaporation?

_____

_____

_____

_____

_____

Investigation 2

Condensation

Materials

- student record sheet on page 40, reproduced for each student
- ice
- water
- food coloring
- glass jars
- large pitcher
- paper towels

Steps to Follow

1. Remind students that in the previous experiment they investigated evaporation—the formation of water vapor.

2. Remind students that when water is warmed, it evaporates and becomes invisible water vapor. Ask them what they think will happen when water vapor is cooled.

3. Prepare a large pitcher of iced water and stir several drops of food coloring into it.

4. Gather students in small groups and distribute a glass jar and a paper towel to each group.

5. Explain that there is water vapor in the air in the classroom, but it can't be seen.

6. Walk around and fill each group's jar about ⅔ full of cold colored water.

7. Invite students to observe the outside of their jars. (Droplets of water will begin to form on the jars.) Students can touch the outside of the jar to feel the moisture. Have them wipe off a few drops on a paper towel to see the color of the drops. (They will be clear.)

8. Ask students why they think the drops on the outside of the jar were clear. Where did the water come from? (Explain that the cold water cooled the air outside the jar, which caused the water vapor in the air to condense on the jar.) Define **condensation** for students.

9. Have students review the processes of evaporation and condensation to see how they are the reverse of one another.

Follow-Up

Repeat the experiment, except this time tape a thermometer to the outside of the glass jars. When water droplets form on the outside of the jar, note the temperature. This temperature is the dew point, a number often used by meteorologists. Dew point is defined as the saturation point of the air—the point at which it can hold no more water. Dew point depends on air temperature.

Condensation

Procedure and Observations

1. Watch the outside of the jar as your teacher pours cold water into it.

2. What did you notice on the outside of the jar several minutes later?

   _____

   _____

3. What difference did you notice between the water in the jar and the other water?

   _____

   _____

Conclusions

4. Why did water form on the outside of the jar?

   _____

   _____

5. Where did the water on the outside of the jar come from?

   _____

6. What is the name for invisible water in the air?

   _____

7. What is condensation?

   _____

   _____

8. What is needed for condensation to occur?

   _____

   _____

Investigation 3

Making Clouds

Materials

See advance preparation on page 34.

- student record sheets on pages 42 and 43, reproduced for each student
- clear plastic 1-liter bottles
- matches
- flashlight
- water

Steps to Follow

1. Review the processes of evaporation and condensation. Ask students what they think happens when water vapor condenses in the sky. Tell them they will do an investigation to find out.

2. Gather students into small groups. Distribute a plastic bottle to each group and have them fill the bottles with about half an inch of water. Have them swirl the water around.

3. As you supervise closely, have them carefully light and drop two or three lit matches into the bottle. Make sure plenty of smoke gets trapped in the bottle. Students should quickly screw the lid on tight. (Water vapor needs to condense onto tiny particles of matter in the air. The smoke particles will serve this purpose.)

4. Turn off the room lights.

5. Have one student shine the flashlight directly into the bottle. Have another student squeeze the bottle in the middle of its sides. The air in the bottle should become fairly clear.

6. Ask the student to release the squeeze. A cloud of water vapor should become visible in the light of the flashlight. Encourage students to repeat this procedure several times.

7. Ask students what they have created inside their bottles (a cloud).

8. Discuss the "ingredients" that are necessary in order to form clouds in the atmosphere (water vapor, dust particles).

Follow-Up

Have students repeat the investigation without first dropping the lit matches into the bottles. What happens? (No cloud forms.) Encourage students to explain their observations. (Water vapor needs particles to condense on.)

Name _____

Making Clouds

Concept

3

Weather

Investigation 3

Procedure and Observations

1. Place a small amount of water in your team's bottle. Drop 2 or 3 lit matches inside and then quickly screw the top on.

2. After your teacher turns the lights off, hold a flashlight up so that it shines through the bottle. Have your partner squeeze the sides of the bottle.

3. What did you observe inside the bottle? Draw and describe your observations.

_____

_____

_____

_____

©2002 by Evan-Moor Corp.   42   Weather • EMC 876

4. Now have your partner release the sides of the bottle.

5. When the bottle was released, what did you observe? Draw and describe your observations.

_____

_____

_____

_____

Conclusions

6. What ingredients are necessary to create a cloud?

_____

7. How do you think clouds are formed in the atmosphere?

_____

_____

_____

Investigation 4

The Water Cycle

Materials

See advance preparation on page 34.

- student record sheet on page 45, reproduced for each student
- crushed ice
- water
- aluminum pie plate
- heavy-duty oven mitt
- glass beaker
- hot plate
- flashlight

Steps to Follow

1. Discuss with students the concepts investigated so far: evaporation, condensation, and cloud formation. Tell them that, with this lesson, they will see how all these processes tie together in nature.

2. Draw a model of the water cycle (see page 35) on the chalkboard, leaving out the arrows and the labels.

3. Show students the materials you will be using for this experiment. Tell them that since a hot plate and hot water will be used, they need to use their best laboratory behavior.

4. Fill a pie tin with water and crushed ice. Place a beaker of water on the hot plate and turn it to "high."

5. Explain that the pie tin filled with crushed ice and water represents the cooler air in the upper atmosphere. The steaming water represents warm, moist air rising from the surface of Earth.

6. Once the water has started boiling, put on the oven mitt and hold the ice-and-water-filled pie plate 2 to 3 feet (0.6 to 0.9 m) above the steam. Have a student turn off the room lights. Have another student shine the flashlight underneath the pie plate.

7. Within a few minutes, students should notice a cloud forming where the warm moist air hits the cooler air under the pan. As more condensation occurs, the air underneath the pie plate becomes saturated. Drops of water will form under the pie plate, and rain will begin to fall as **precipitation.**

8. Once students return to their seats, discuss all the elements of the water cycle (evaporation, condensation, precipitation) and relate them to this demonstration. Introduce the term **water cycle,** and explain that the water cycle describes how water moves from Earth's surface into the air, and then back to the surface again. Have students complete their record sheets.

9. Add arrows to the water cycle illustration you made on the chalkboard earlier and have student volunteers add the labels.

The Water Cycle

Procedure and Observations

1. Watch as your teacher performs the water cycle demonstration.

2. Label each part of the water cycle model as demonstrated. Use the water cycle words to fill in the blanks.

Water Cycle Words: evaporation   condensation   precipitation

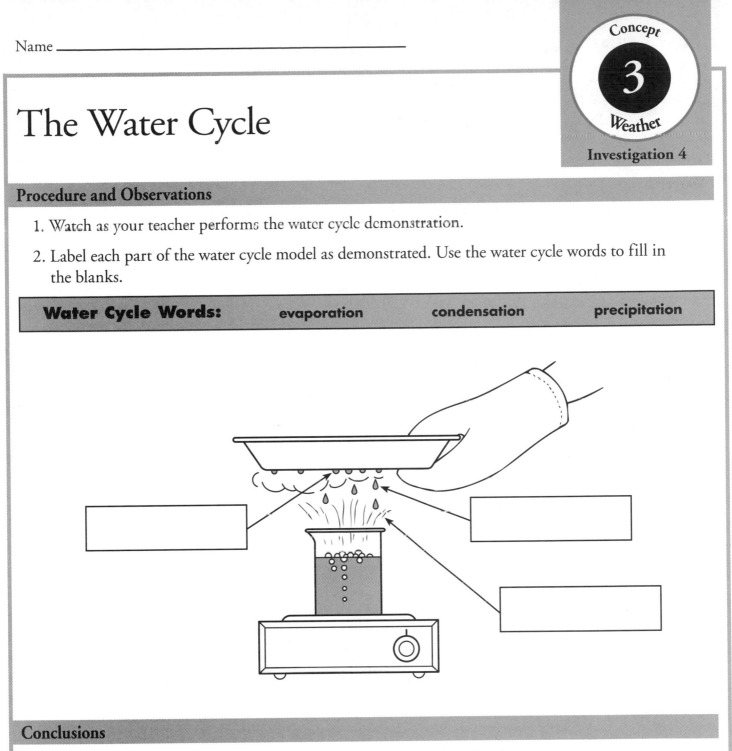

Conclusions

3. What ingredients were needed to make a water cycle model in the classroom?

_____

_____

_____

4. On the back of this sheet, draw a model of the water cycle as it would occur in nature. Use the water cycle words. Include the Sun, a large body of water like the ocean, and mountains in your model. Use arrows to indicate how water moves through the water cycle.

Clouds directly affect weather.

Prepare in Advance

Investigation 1: Have students help you cut "windows" in 4" x 6" index cards so that the card becomes a frame with a half-inch border all around. Each student will need one card.

Investigation 2: You may want to locate a color cloud chart to supplement the black and white one provided on the next page. In addition to science supply stores, you might try searching some weather sites on the Internet. (See page 15.)

Teacher Information

The **tendency** of clouds is defined as whether cloud coverage is increasing or decreasing. Tendency is often associated with other weather observations, including wind, humidity, and air pressure. This combination of factors is part of what meteorologists look at when making weather forecasts. Observing cloud types and tendencies is a good way to start making forecasts.

There are four main types of clouds: cumulus, cumulonimbus, cirrus, and stratus.

Cumulus clouds usually arrive after a storm. Or they may build up on a spring or summer afternoon. They can bring scattered showers, but they often indicate that fair weather is arriving.

Cumulonimbus clouds typically mean thunderstorms with heavy rain. In extreme cases, high winds, hail, and even tornadoes may drop out of these clouds.

Cirrus clouds are fair weather clouds. But they can indicate a storm is on the horizon, especially if they are blowing in from the west.

Stratus clouds are low clouds that bring drizzle, rain, and fog. They may last all day; in coastal areas, they often burn off in the late morning or afternoon.

Often, there is more than one type of cloud in the sky. Also, there are variations, or sub-categories, of these four main types of clouds. Clouds that form at high altitudes begin with a "cirr." Medium altitude clouds start with "alto." "Cumu" means that the clouds are heaped up. "Strat" means the clouds are shaped like a sheet. Sometimes these characteristics are combined, producing such cloud types as stratocumulus, altostratus, cirrocumulus, and altocumulus.

Cloud Types

Cloud	Altitude	Description	Associated Weather
Cirrus	12,000 m and up	Wispy and see-through	Typical quiet winter weather; first sign of an approaching storm
Cumulonimbus	1,500 to 15,000 m	Large, billowing, mushroom-like	Thunderstorms, heavy rain, and hail; possible tornadoes in the Midwest and Southeast
Cumulus	1,500 to 6,000 m	Puffy, like cotton balls	Clearing weather; follows a storm
Stratus	0 to 1,500 m	Gray layers	Drizzle, fog, or overcast; usually follows a storm

Investigation 1

Cloud Coverage and Tendency

Materials

See advance preparation on page 46.

- student record sheets on pages 49 and 50, reproduced for each student

- *Daily Weather Chart* on page 16

- 4″ x 6″ (8 x 15 cm) index cards, with "windows" cut out

- pencils

Steps to Follow

1. Go over the terms *increase* and *decrease* with your class. Explain that meteorologists use these terms to describe the **tendency** of cloud coverage in the sky: Clouds are said to be increasing or decreasing.

2. Distribute a record sheet and a prepared index card "window" to each student. Take the class outside.

3. Have the students observe the sky and the amount of clouds there are. Would they describe the sky as cloudy, partly cloudy, or clear?

4. One way to observe cloud coverage is to pretend you are looking out a window. Invite students to sit down and observe a location in the sky through their "windows."

5. Point out the gridded rectangle on students' record sheets. Have students sketch a picture of their part of the sky inside the rectangle.

6. Bring students back inside.

7. Have students estimate what percentage of the sky is covered by clouds. They can do this by counting the number of squares that fall within the drawn clouds on the grid. Have students add together partially-covered squares to make whole numbers. To determine what percentage of the sky is covered, have students compare the number of squares covered by clouds to those not covered.

8. Repeat this activity several hours later. Students should observe from the same locations.

9. Again, have students calculate the cloud coverage as a percentage (for example, 52 percent coverage). Ask students if the cloud coverage increased, decreased, or stayed the same from one observation to the next. Have them use the word **tendency** in their reports.

10. Assign classroom weather monitors to determine cloud coverage percentages twice a day for the next several weeks, and to record the data on the *Daily Weather Chart*. Weather monitors should also record whether clouds are increasing or decreasing.

Name _____

Cloud Coverage and Tendency

Procedure and Observations

1. Go outside with your class and observe the sky.

2. Sketch the clouds you see through your "window" on the grid below.

   ### Observation Date and Time:

   _____

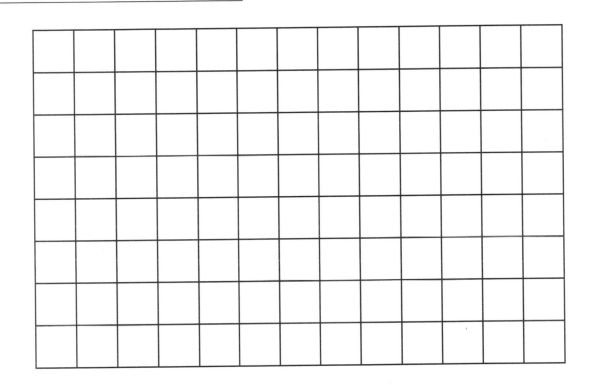

3. How many squares are covered by clouds? (Add together partially-covered squares to make whole numbers.)

   _____

4. How many are not covered?

   _____

5. What percentage of the sky is covered by clouds?

   _____

6. Later in the day, make your sky observations again. Sketch the clouds you see through your "window" on the grid below.

Observation Date and Time:

_____

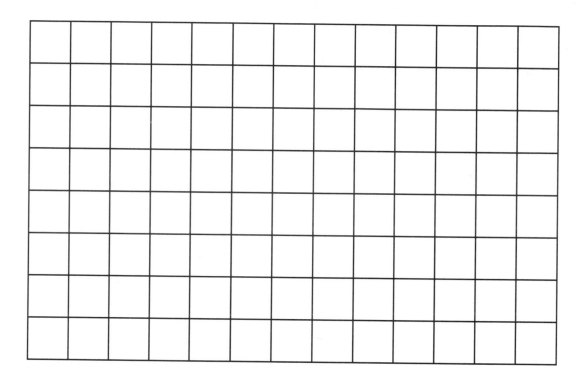

7. How many squares are covered by clouds? (Add together partially-covered squares to make whole numbers.)

_____

8. How many squares are not covered?

_____

9. What percentage of the sky is covered by clouds?

_____

Conclusion

10. What was the cloud tendency over the course of the day?

_____

Concept 4 Weather

Investigation 2

Cloud Types

Materials

See advance preparation on page 46.

- student record sheets on pages 52 and 53, reproduced for each student

- overhead transparency of the *Cloud Types* chart on page 47

- *Daily Weather Chart* on page 16

- 11″ x 17″ (28 x 43 cm) light blue construction paper

- rulers

- glue

- cotton balls

- tissue paper

- pencils

- cloud chart (See advance preparation for instructions.)

Steps to Follow

1. Using the *Cloud Types* transparency, go over the different types of clouds with students. Explain the characteristics of each cloud and the altitude the clouds are typically found at in the sky. Remind students that there is often more than one type of cloud in the sky at any one time.

2. Bring students outside and have them observe the sky. Which types of clouds do they see now?

3. Have students make their own cloud charts. Instruct them to divide a sheet of 11″ x 17″ (28 x 43 cm) construction paper into four sections by folding the paper into four quadrants and then using a ruler to draw lines along the folds.

4. In each of the four boxes on the chart, have students write the cloud name, altitude range, and other general information. Then invite them to add cloud models to their charts. Encourage them to make their cloud models three-dimensional by using such materials as modified cotton balls, tissue paper, and so on. Remind students to base their models on what each of the cloud types actually looks like. Have them refer to the transparency or another cloud chart as needed.

5. When students have completed their cloud charts, review with them the four types of clouds. You may want to post the charts next to the *Daily Weather Chart*.

6. Have students observe and draw cloud types they see over the next three days. Have them record their data on their record sheets.

7. Have weather monitors observe cloud types twice daily for the next several weeks. Have them add their data to the *Daily Weather Chart*.

Follow-Up

Several variations of the four main cloud types exist. Use a cloud chart or pictures to identify the other types of clouds. Weather monitors can start including these other types of clouds in their weather chart updates as well.

Cloud Types

Procedure and Observations

1. Go outside and observe different cloud types with your class.

2. Label each box below with one of the four cloud types and draw a small picture of the cloud in the box.

Cloud _____   **Cloud** _____

Cloud _____   **Cloud** _____

3. At what elevation is each of the four cloud types usually found?

Cloud Type	Altitude (m)
Cirrus	
Cumulus	
Cumulonimbus	
Stratus	

4. Observe the clouds for the next three days. Draw the cloud types you see each day in the spaces below.

Day 1

Day 2

Day 3

Concept 4 Weather

Investigation 3

Forecasting with Clouds

Materials

- student record sheet on page 55, reproduced for each student
- *Daily Weather Chart* on page 16
- student cloud charts

Steps to Follow

1. Have students look again at the cloud charts they completed in Investigation 2.

2. Review with students the different types of weather associated with each of the four types of clouds. (See Teacher Information on page 46.) Cirrus clouds are often associated with quiet weather. Cumulonimbus clouds bring heavy rains, and even tornadoes. Cumulus clouds often follow storms and indicate fair weather. Stratus clouds bring drizzle, fog, and light rain. They sometimes burn off in the afternoon.

3. Tell students that they can make predictions about coming weather based on the types of clouds they observe and the tendency of the cloud coverage. For example, if there are cumulonimbus clouds that are increasing in size and sky coverage, students could predict a chance of showers or thunderstorms arriving soon. If there are cumulus clouds that seem to be decreasing, or going away, the simple prediction could be partly cloudy this afternoon, but mostly fair weather.

4. Distribute the record sheets. Explain that students will use the sheets to practice making weather predictions based on cloud observations. Go over students' predictions as a class once they have completed the exercise. The following day, have students review their predictions and see if they were right. Hold a class discussion of which predictions were most accurate and why.

5. Have students start adding "predictions" to the *Daily Weather Chart* based on their observations of cloud types and coverage. For example, if there are cirrus clouds that cover about 20 percent of the sky, and cloud coverage is neither increasing nor decreasing, a reasonable prediction could be "fair weather." On the other hand, if there are stratus clouds that are covering 75 percent of the sky, and cloud coverage is increasing, a reasonable prediction could be fog or drizzle with mostly cloudy skies.

Follow-Up

Have your class compare their forecasts with local forecasts available through the Internet, including the National Weather Service and The Weather Channel (see page 15). Both of these sites have local and national links with forecasts. Also check local television weathercasts for their predictions.

Name _____

Forecasting with Clouds

Procedure and Observations

1. What types of clouds are in the sky today? Check once in the morning and once in the afternoon.

Time of Day	Cloud Type or Types
Morning	
Afternoon	

2. Did cloud coverage increase or decrease during the course of the day?

_____

3. How would you describe the weather overall right now?

_____

_____

Conclusions

4. Based on your observations of clouds and cloud tendency, what do you think the weather will be like later today? Record your prediction below.

_____

_____

5. What do you think the weather will be like tomorrow?

_____

_____

6. Were your predictions correct? Why or why not?

_____

_____

_____

Climate is affected by Earth's features.

Prepare in Advance

Investigation 2: Mark the cities of Singapore (1°N), Calcutta (23°N), Washington, D.C. (39°N), and Moscow (56°N) on a world map.

Investigation 3: For each group of students, fill one coffee can with sand and push a thermometer down into the sand. Tape a thermometer inside another coffee can and fill this can with water. Place all cans in the refrigerator several hours before the investigation begins.

Investigation 4: Use the Internet to search for precipitation averages for pairs of cities. One of the cities should be on the west side of a mountain range, and the other city should be on the east side of the same mountain range. The cities should be near each other. Precipitation differences between paired cities is enhanced west of the Rocky Mountains. Seattle and Yakima, Sacramento and Reno, and Los Angeles and Palm Springs are good examples. Plot these cities on a physical map of North America to show the class.

Teacher Information

Within the troposphere, the lowest level of Earth's atmosphere, air temperature decreases with altitude at a constant rate—about 3°F for every 1,000 feet of elevation. The air is thinner, or less dense, at higher altitudes than it is at sea level. Because there are fewer molecules to absorb the Sun's radiation, the overall temperature is lower. This explains why we can see snow-capped mountains from the relative warmth of an alpine valley.

Latitude, the north-and-south distance from the equator, affects the overall temperature of an area. The closer a location is to the equator, the more year-round direct sunlight it receives, and the warmer it is relative to locations farther north and south. Latitude also determines whether or not an area will experience any seasonal variations of temperatures. Earth is tilted approximately 23° on its axis. As a result, the amount of direct sunlight that falls on a particular place varies from season to season. The Northern Hemisphere gets more direct sunlight during our summer, making it warmer overall from June through September. The opposite happens in the Southern Hemisphere. Its summer occurs during the Northern Hemisphere's winter—December through March. Areas near the equator don't experience as much seasonal variation in temperature because they receive a fairly constant amount of direct sunlight throughout the year.

Water absorbs and releases heat more slowly than land does. As a result, ocean temperatures are fairly constant, and so are areas near the ocean—such as beach communities. These areas are often referred to as having "oceanic climates." Land heats up and cools down faster than water. As a result, land-locked areas experience greater ranges of temperatures than areas in oceanic climates. Areas far from large bodies of water are often referred to as having "continental climates."

Earth's rotation causes the prevailing winds to move generally from west to east across the United States. As the winds move across the Pacific Ocean, they pick up moisture. As the winds move east and run into mountains, they are forced upward, where the air is cooler. Since cooler air can hold less moisture than warmer air, moisture being carried by the winds condenses into clouds. Eventually, the clouds give up their moisture through precipitation. Once the winds finally reach the tops of the mountains, they start dropping back down the eastern side. As the elevation decreases, air temperature increases. Warm air can hold more moisture, so precipitation decreases substantially. In many cases, the eastern slope is actually dried out by the descending winds. The result is that western slopes of mountains typically receive abundant precipitation. The eastern slopes, on the other hand, are in what's known as a **rain shadow,** and they receive much less precipitation.

A perfect example of the rain shadow effect can be seen in the Olympic Mountains of northwestern Washington. Up to 200 (508 cm) inches of precipitation falls annually on the west side of Mount Olympus, while only 20 inches (51 cm) of rain falls in the town of Sequim, which is located in the rain shadow to the east.

Elevation and Temperature Data, Lake Tahoe and Sacramento

Sample Summer Temperatures in Lake Tahoe and Sacramento, CA

City	Elevation (ft)	Temperature (°F)
Sacramento, CA	25	100
	1,000	97
	2,000	94
	3,000	91
	4,000	88
	5,000	85
Lake Tahoe, CA	6,200	82

Sample Winter Temperatures in Lake Tahoe and Sacramento, CA

City	Elevation (ft)	Temperature (°F)
Sacramento, CA	25	50
	1,000	47
	2,000	44
	3,000	41
	4,000	38
	5,000	35
Lake Tahoe, CA	6,200	32

Four World Cities

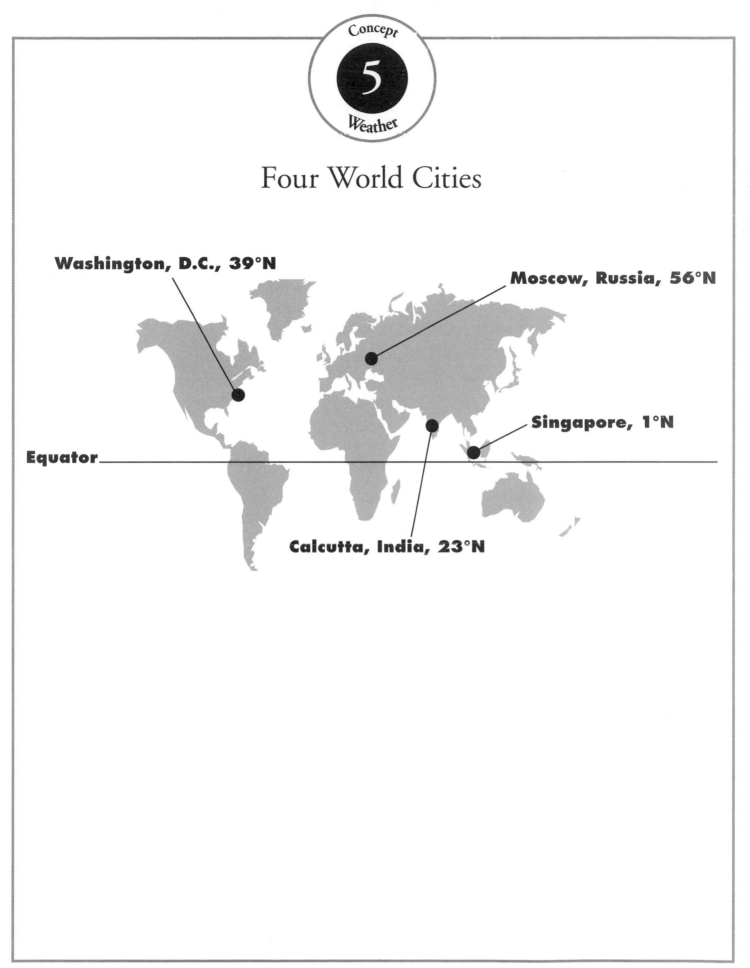

Washington, D.C., 39°N

Moscow, Russia, 56°N

Singapore, 1°N

Equator

Calcutta, India, 23°N

Temperature Data for Four World Cities

Average Monthly Mean Temperatures for Four Cities (°F)

Month	Singapore (1° North Latitude)	Calcutta, India (23° North Latitude)	Washington, D.C. (39° North Latitude)	Moscow, Russia (56° North Latitude)
January	80	67	36	12
February	80	71	37	15
March	81	80	46	24
April	82	85	55	38
May	82	86	65	53
June	81	85	74	62
July	81	84	78	66
August	81	83	76	63
September	81	83	70	52
October	81	81	58	40
November	80	73	48	28
December	80	67	38	17
Yearly Average	81	79	57	39

Sunlight and Latitude

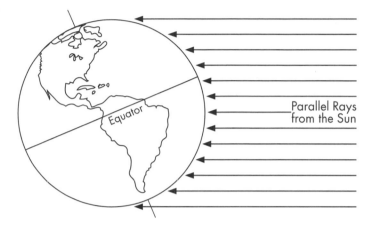

Parallel Rays
from the Sun

Winter in the Northern Hemisphere

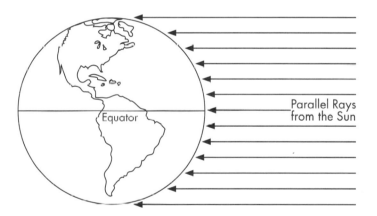

Parallel Rays
from the Sun

Spring and Fall

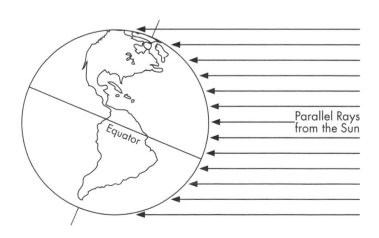

Parallel Rays
from the Sun

Summer in the Northern Hemisphere

Five U.S. Cities with Temperature Data

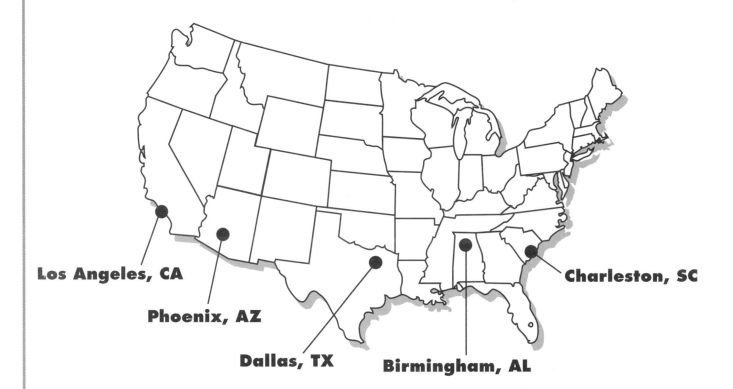

Data for Five Cities

Location	Elevation (ft)	Latitude	Mean Temperature (°F)		
			January	July	Average Range
Los Angeles, CA	330	34°N	56	69	
Phoenix, AZ	1,090	33°N	52	92	
Dallas, TX	512	33°N	44	86	
Birmingham, AL	604	33°N	43	80	
Charleston, SC	0	33°N	48	80	

Rain Shadow Effect

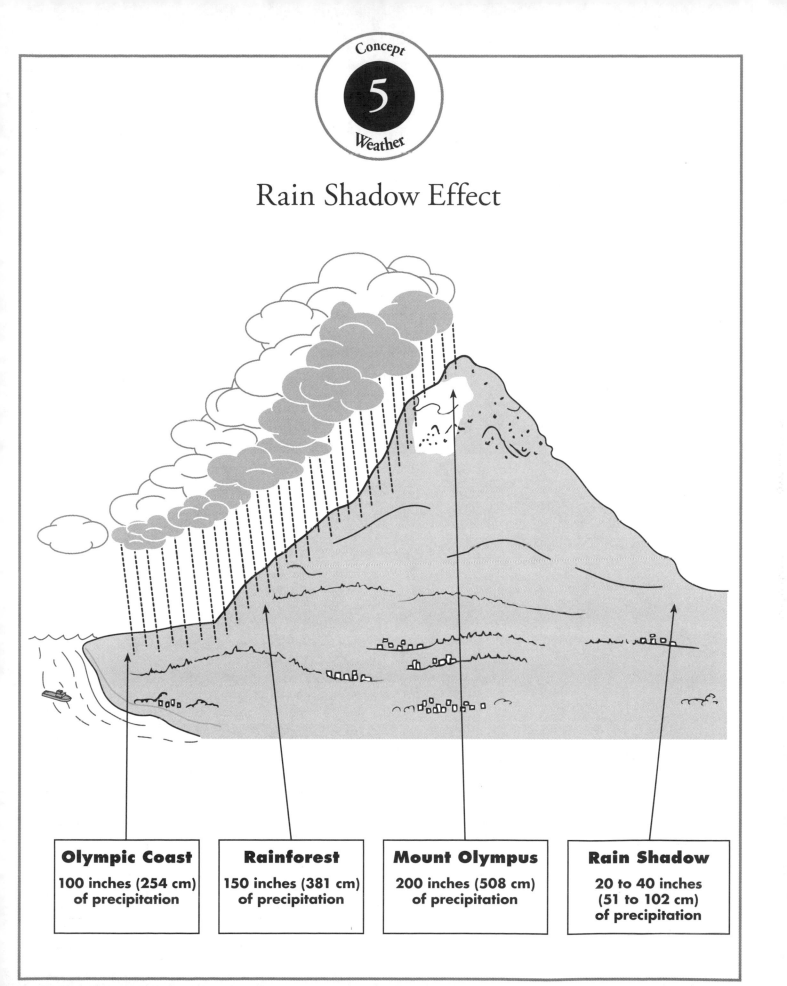

Olympic Coast	**Rainforest**	**Mount Olympus**	**Rain Shadow**
100 inches (254 cm) of precipitation	150 inches (381 cm) of precipitation	200 inches (508 cm) of precipitation	20 to 40 inches (51 to 102 cm) of precipitation

Concept 5 Weather

Investigation 1
Elevation and Temperature

Materials

- student record sheet on page 65, reproduced for each student

- overhead transparency of *Elevation and Temperature Data, Lake Tahoe and Sacramento* on page 58

- physical map of California

Steps to Follow

1. Review with students the concept of **elevation.** Explain that cities on the ocean are at sea level, but that those located inland may be higher than sea level, especially if they are located in the mountains.

2. Show the class the overhead transparency of summer and winter temperatures in Sacramento and Lake Tahoe. Explain that Lake Tahoe is an area in the Sierra Nevada mountains of California. Sacramento is located in California's Central Valley. If you have a physical map of California, show it to students.

3. Ask students if they notice any pattern in the data. (Students should notice that as elevation increases, temperature decreases.)

4. Explain that the higher the elevation, the cooler the air becomes. For every 1,000 foot rise in elevation, there is approximately a 3°F drop in temperature.

5. Tell students that if they know the temperature of a town located at one elevation, they can estimate the temperature of a nearby town that is located at a higher elevation. Have your class add to the tables by estimating the summer and winter temperatures of a town near Lake Tahoe that is at 8,000 feet, and one that is at 9,000 feet.

6. As an exercise, draw a picture of your city on the board and include in the drawing a nearby city in the mountains. Give a sample temperature in degrees Fahrenheit (°F) for your city. Then challenge students to determine the approximate temperature of the other city based on the 3°F per 1,000 feet elevation rule. Give both summer and winter sample data.

Follow-Up

Look up on the Internet the temperatures of two local cities, one that is at a lower elevation and one at a higher elevation. (Try The Weather Channel, www.weather.com, and the National Weather Service, www.nws.noaa.gov.) On a bar graph, plot the temperatures of both cities each day for several days. Compare the temperature differences with the 3°F per 1,000 feet temperature formula. Is the formula accurate? What might make the formula vary?

Name _____

Elevation and Temperature

Procedure and Observations

1. Look at the temperature data for Sacramento and Lake Tahoe in the summer. What pattern do you notice in the data?

   _____

   _____

   _____

2. Round the elevations of Sacramento and Lake Tahoe to the nearest 1,000 ft. What can you say about how temperature changes as you move up 1,000 ft in elevation?

   _____

   _____

3. Based on the formula you just came up with for temperature change and elevation, what would Lake Tahoe's temperature be when it's 105°F in Sacramento?

   _____

   _____

4. Estimate Lake Tahoe's temperature when it's 48°F in Sacramento.

   _____

   _____

Conclusion

5. What is the relationship between elevation and temperature?

   _____

   _____

   _____

Investigation 2

Latitude and Temperature

Materials

See advance preparation on page 56.

- student record sheet on page 67, reproduced for each student
- overhead transparency of *Four World Cities* on page 59
- overhead transparency of *Temperature Data for Four World Cities* on page 60
- overhead transparency of *Sunlight and Latitude* on page 61
- world map

Steps to Follow

1. Show the class the *Four World Cities* transparency. (You may also want to point the cities out on a classroom world map.) Identify each city's latitude in degrees. Go over the concept of **latitude** with students. Use the world map to walk them through latitude readings from the equator to the poles.

2. Now show the class the *Temperature Data for Four World Cities* transparency. Have students note the temperatures during each season.

3. For each city, have students calculate the **temperature range,** or the difference between the highest and lowest temperature. Have them record their data on their record sheets.

4. Ask students if they notice any connection between latitude and temperature range. (Students may notice that the farther away a city is from the equator, the cooler its average temperature is, and the greater its seasonal temperature range.)

5. Show students the *Sunlight and Latitude* transparency.

6. Explain that the areas of the world that receive the most direct sunlight are usually the warmest places on Earth. Since the equator, which is at 0°N latitude, receives the most direct sunlight throughout the year, it is usually the warmest region of our planet. As you move farther north and south in latitude toward the poles, the overall temperature becomes cooler.

7. Use the overhead to explain the concept of seasons. Because Earth is tilted on its axis, higher latitudes in both the Northern and Southern Hemispheres experience great differences in temperature between summer and winter. Areas near the equator do not.

Follow-Up

Have students use the Internet to research temperature data for two major cities in the Southern Hemisphere with different latitudes. Instruct students to prepare a graph of the monthly temperatures, then calculate the temperature range. These graphs and data can be presented to the class.

Name _____

Latitude and Temperature

Procedure and Observations

1. Look at the world map below and the locations of the four cities.

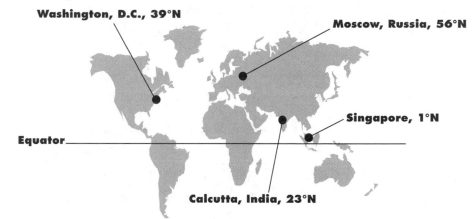

Washington, D.C., 39°N

Moscow, Russia, 56°N

Singapore, 1°N

Equator

Calcutta, India, 23°N

2. Look at the *Temperature Data for Four World Cities* transparency.

3. How do the average temperatures of the cities change as latitude increases?

_____

_____

4. What is the seasonal range of temperatures for

Singapore: _____

Calcutta: _____

Washington, D.C.: _____

Moscow: _____

Conclusion

5. Based on the data you saw, what conclusion can you draw about how average temperature and temperature range change with latitude?

_____

_____

_____

Investigation 3

Water and Temperature

Materials

See advance preparation on page 56.

- student record sheets on pages 70 and 71, reproduced for each student
- overhead transparency of *Five U.S. Cities with Temperature Data* on page 62
- map of the United States
- coffee cans
- water
- sand
- thermometers
- erasable markers

Steps to Follow

1. Show students the *Five U.S. Cities with Temperature Data* transparency.

2. Have students find the average temperature range for each city by subtracting the January temperature from the July temperature. Have them record the data on their record sheets.

3. Using the erasable markers, write the temperature ranges next to the average monthly mean temperatures for each city on the transparency.

Data for Five Cities

Location	Elevation (ft)	Latitude	Mean Temperature (°F)		
			January	July	Average Range
Los Angeles, CA	330	34°N	56	69	
Phoenix, AZ	1,090	33°N	52	92	
Dallas, TX	512	33°N	44	86	
Birmingham, AL	604	33°N	43	80	
Charleston, SC	0	33°N	48	80	

4. Ask students to compare the temperature ranges of the cities located on the coast (Los Angeles and Charleston) to those located inland (Phoenix, Dallas, and Birmingham). Which city's temperature varies the most between the seasons (Dallas)? Which varies the least (Los Angeles)?

5. Ask the class why they think the cities have different average temperature ranges. (Possible responses might include elevation, latitude, and proximity to water.)

6. Point out that each of the five cities is located at approximately the same latitude, so they all get about the same amount of direct sunlight. The elevation of each city is also similar, and none are in the mountains.

7. Explain to your class that earlier in the day, you placed coffee cans in the refrigerator, and that half the cans were filled with water and the others were filled with sand.

8. Divide the class into small groups. Take the coffee cans out of the refrigerator and give one can filled with water and one can filled with sand to each group of students. They should quickly read and record the temperatures. (The temperatures should be about the same.)

9. Have the groups take their coffee cans outside and put in them in sunlight, leaving the thermometers in place. Ask students what they think will happen to the temperatures of each.

10. Have groups check and record the temperatures of each can at 15-minute intervals for an hour. Tell them to record their data on their record sheets.

11. Hold a class discussion of the results. Which can heated up the fastest: the one with the sand, or the one with the water? (The one with sand heated faster.)

12. Challenge students to relate what they learned in this experiment to the temperature range data they looked at earlier.

13. Explain that land heats up faster than water, so areas surrounded by land have greater temperature ranges than areas near water. Since water is slower to heat up, areas near large bodies of water have smaller temperature ranges.

14. Lead students to conclude that Los Angeles's small temperature range is due to its close proximity to the Pacific Ocean, while land-locked Dallas experiences greater temperature fluctuations.

Follow-Up

The reverse effect happens at night. Land cools off faster. This can be demonstrated by placing the can of sand and the can of water back in the refrigerator. Check and record the temperatures at 15-minute intervals for an hour to see which can cools first.

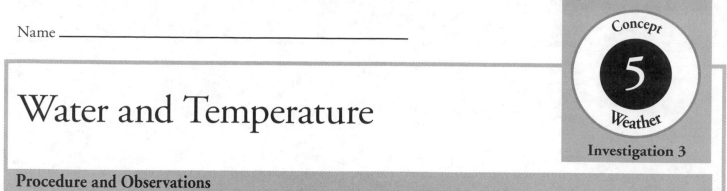

Water and Temperature

Concept

5

Weather

Investigation 3

Procedure and Observations

1. Look at the location of the five cities on the map below.

2. Record the average July and January temperatures for each city. Then find the temperature range for each city by subtracting the January temperature from the July temperature.

	Los Angeles, CA	Phoenix, AZ	Dallas, TX	Birmingham, AL	Charleston, SC
July					
January					
Range					

3. Why do you think the five cities have different average temperature ranges?

_____

_____

_____

4. Record the temperatures of the can of water and the can of sand at 15-minute intervals for an hour.

	Temperatures (°F)				
	Start	After 15 Minutes	After 30 Minutes	After 45 Minutes	After 1 Hour
Can of Water					
Can of Sand					

5. Which coffee can heated up faster?

_____

Conclusions

6. What connection can you make between the coffee can experiment and the temperature range data for the five U.S. cities?

_____

_____

_____

_____

7. Why does Los Angeles have the smallest temperature range?

_____

_____

_____

8. Why does Dallas have the greatest temperature range?

_____

_____

_____

Concept 5 Weather

Investigation 4

Mountains and Precipitation

Materials

See *advance preparation* on page 56.

- student record sheet on page 73, reproduced for each student
- overhead transparency of the *Rain Shadow Effect* on page 63
- physical map of North America
- precipitation data for three pairs of cities

Steps to Follow

1. Show the class the three pairs of cities you have marked on the map of North America. (See "Prepare in Advance" on page 56.) Write the precipitation data you collected for each city on the board. Have students record the data on the table on their record sheets.

2. Ask students to speculate as to why the precipitation data varies so greatly for each pair of cities, even though they are so close on the map.

3. Using the *Rain Shadow Effect* transparency, explain how moisture precipitates out of the air as it moves up and over mountains.

4. Now ask students to explain why the cities in each pair receive the amount of precipitation that they do. (Students should be able to identify the cities on the wet western slopes v. the dry eastern slopes.)

Follow-Up

Ask the class why they think Los Angeles gets less rain than the Olympic Mountains in Washington, even though they are both west of the mountains. Answers might include: steepness of the mountains, location on the western slope, proximity to the ocean, and that Washington is farther north and on a more active storm path.

Name _____

Mountains and Precipitation

Procedure and Observations

1. Look at the physical map of North America your teacher is holding. Locate the pairs of cities marked on the map.

2. Record the names of the cities and a description of their geographic locations on the table below. Enter the precipitation data your teacher provides.

	City Name	Annual Precipitation (in. or cm)	Description of Geographic Location
First Pair	1.		
	2.		
Second Pair	1.		
	2.		
Third Pair	1.		
	2.		

3. Which three cities get the most precipitation?

_____

4. Which three cities get the least precipitation?

_____

Conclusions

5. What pattern do you notice in the precipitation data?

_____

_____

6. Explain what causes the pattern you see.

_____

_____

Local weather conditions can be used to forecast weather.

Prepare in Advance

Investigation 1: Record different television weather forecasts, including one from The Weather Channel. Gather three or more newspaper weather maps, including one from a local newspaper and one from *USA Today*. Bookmark several Internet weather sites on your school computer, including The Weather Channel (www.weather.com), the National Weather Service (www.nws.noaa.gov), and Accuweather (www1.accuweather.com).

Teacher Information

Weather reports on television and in the newspaper typically contain information about current conditions and include temperature, wind speed, wind direction, barometric pressure, and cloud coverage/sky conditions. They usually also report the high and low temperatures for the day. Satellite pictures and radar maps show moisture and other forms of weather moving across an area.

Weather maps like the one shown below summarize the various weather conditions occurring in an area. Symbols are used to represent various aspects of weather, including precipitation, cloud coverage, barometric pressure, wind direction, and movement of fronts (masses of warm or cold air). Symbols allow a great deal of information to be presented clearly in a small space.

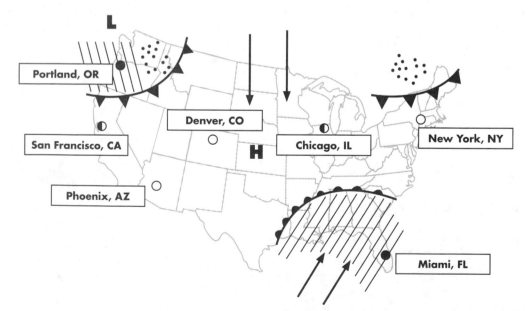

Meteorologists use a combination of information to generate forecasts. Weather spotters give reports of up-to-the-minute current conditions in a number of different locations within a region. Computer models use this data, together with seasonal averages, to project upcoming changes in weather.

Weather Symbols

Weather	Symbol	Weather	Symbol
Rain	//////	Low Pressure	Ⓛ
Snow	⠒⠒⠒	Wind Direction	↑
Clear	○	Cold Front	▲___
Partly Cloudy	◐	Warm Front	●___
Cloudy	●	Occluded Front	▲●___
High Pressure	Ⓗ	Stationary Front	▼●___

Types of Fronts

Cold Front: where a mass of cold air is replacing a mass of warm air.

Warm Front: where a mass of warm air is replacing a mass of cold air.

Occluded Front: forms where a cold front overtakes a warm front.

Stationary Front: a cold front or warm front that shows little or no movement.

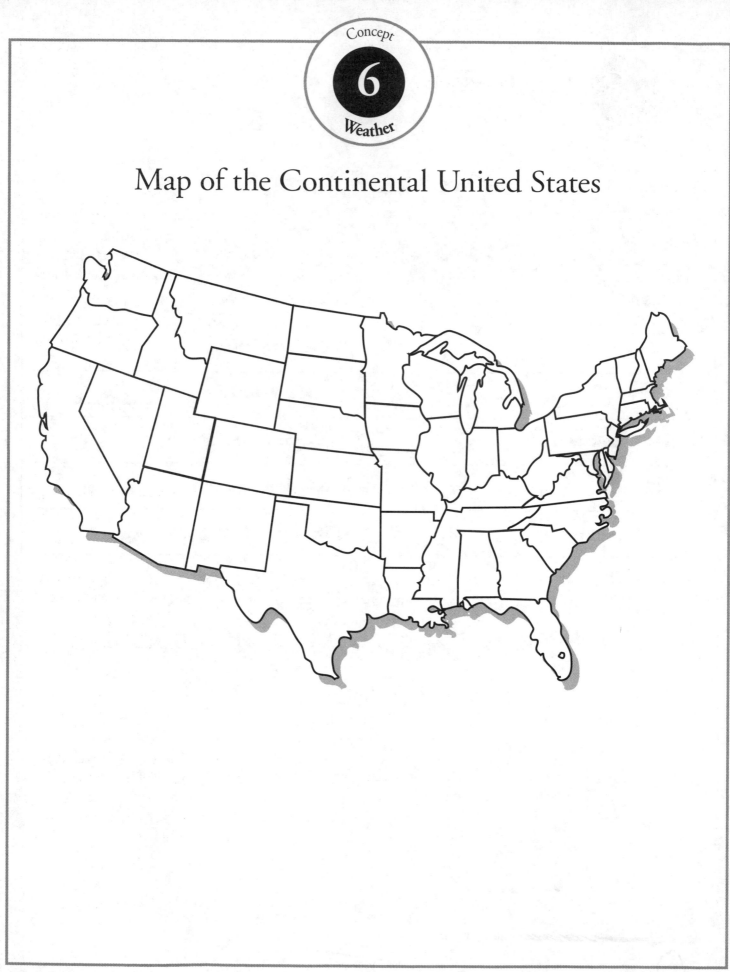

Map of the Continental United States

Concept
6
Weather

Investigation 1
Weather Maps

Materials

See advance preparation on page 74.

- student record sheet on page 78, reproduced for each student
- overhead transparency of *Weather Symbols* on page 75
- overhead transparency of *Map of the Continental United States* on page 76
- copies of the *Map of the Continental United States,* reproduced for each student
- weather maps from newspaper
- recorded television weathercasts, local and national
- erasable markers

Steps to Follow

1. Ask students if they have ever looked at the weather page in the newspaper or watched a television weathercast. Talk with your class about the types of information covered in these reports and make a list on the board (temperature, wind speed, wind direction, barometric pressure, cloud coverage/sky conditions, and so on).

2. Show the class the newspaper weather report and the television weathercast. If the class noticed information that wasn't included in the list you made on the board, add that information to the list.

3. Using the *Map of the Continental United States* transparency, model for students how to fill out a weather map by adding information from the newspaper to the U.S. map. Stay with basic weather information at first, such as high temperatures, cloud conditions, and wind direction for 5 to 10 cities.

4. After writing this information on the map, ask students for suggestions on how to make the map look less cluttered. Someone will likely suggest using symbols.

5. Using the *Weather Symbols* transparency, share with students the basic weather symbols for high pressure, low pressure, cold fronts, warm fronts, rain, snow, wind direction, and cloud coverage. Redo the class map using these symbols.

6. Describe the completed weather map to the class as if you are giving a weather report.

7. Using the *Weather Symbols* transparency, have students complete the weather map exercise on their record sheets.

8. Now distribute a copy of the *Map of the Continental United States* to each student. Assign students a particular region of the country and have them fill out their own individual weather maps with temperatures, cold and warm fronts, wind direction, wind speed, precipitation, and barometric pressure for their regions. The weather information should be accurate, so have students use weather Internet sources, as well as television weathercasts and newspaper weather reports. They should date their maps as well and use the weather symbols you introduced.

9. Once students have completed their maps, they can use them to give weather reports to the class.

Name _____

Weather Maps

Procedure and Observations

1. Look at the following weather map of the United States.

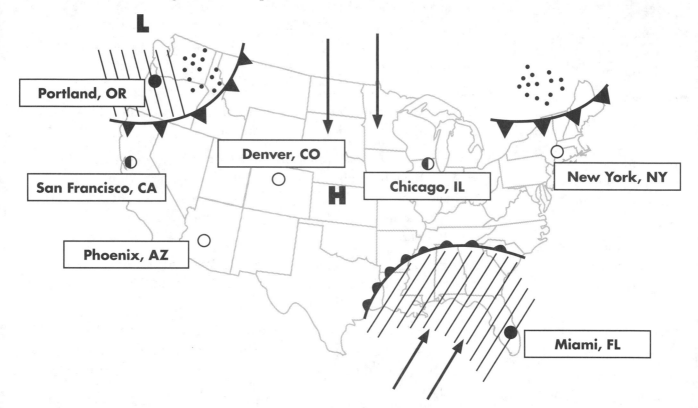

2. Use the data provided to describe the weather in each of the cities listed on the chart.

City	Weather
Portland, OR	
San Francisco, CA	
Phoenix, AZ	
Denver, CO	
Chicago, IL	
Miami, FL	
New York, NY	

Investigation 2

Weather Reporter

Materials

- student record sheet on page 80, reproduced for each student
- recorded television weathercasts, local and national

Steps to Follow

1. Show several more videos of television weathercasts. List and review the maps and information the weathercaster used.

2. Divide students into groups of two. Tell each team that they are going to prepare and present a weather report, complete with a forecast, over the next week or so.

3. Explain that reports should include a series of charts describing current weather conditions (temperature, wind direction, wind speed, cloud coverage/sky conditions, and pressure), today's high and low temperatures, radar information, satellite images, tomorrow's forecast, and the extended forecast. Have students design and decorate these charts so they look like those used on television.

4. Review where students can go to get data for each map, such the weather Internet sites, various newspapers, and television.

5. Assign one group to each day for the next several days. Begin with tomorrow so that today can be spent preparing to research and write.

6. Instruct student pairs to write a script of what they will say during their reports as they present their charts and maps. Remind them that they shouldn't just read what is on the charts and maps; they should make an engaging presentation.

7. Have students practice their reports on one another before presenting them to the class.

Follow-Up

Consider videotaping students' weathercasts and making full news reports. The videotapes can be sent home with students, or presented to parents on open-house night.

Weather Reporter

Procedure and Observations

1. What sorts of information are presented in weather reports?

_____

_____

_____

_____

2. Name two or more ways you can acquire weather data for your weather reports.

_____

_____

_____

_____

Conclusions

3. How do television weathercasters prepare and deliver weathercasts?

_____

_____

_____

4. Why is it a good idea to write down a script and practice your weather report ahead of time?

_____

_____

_____

_____